S is for Sunflower

A Kansas Alphabet

Written by Devin and Corey Scillian and Illustrated by Doug Bowles

Sleeping Bear Press™

2395 South Parkway, Ste. 200
Ann Arbor, MI 48104
www.sleepingbearpress.com

Printed and bound in the United States.

11 10 9

Library of Congress Cataloging-in-Publication Data

Scillian, Devin.
S is for sunflower : a Kansas alphabet / written by Devin and Corey Scillian;
illustrated by Doug Bowles.
p. cm.
ISBN 978-1-58536-061-1
1. Kansas—Juvenile literature. 2. English language—Alphabet—Juvenile
literature. I. Scillian, Corey. II. Bowles, Doug. III. Title.
F681.3.S38 2004
978.1—dc22   2004005956

For Beth, Ed, and Matt, and in loving memory of Terri.

DEVIN & COREY

&

To Bet, Lauren, and Adam, my loving family,
who always support and inspire me.

And a special thanks to my rep Helen,
and my friends at Sleeping Bear Press,
who gave me this great creative opportunity!

DOUG

Let's meet in the middle and don't be late.
I'll meet you in the Sunflower State,
where waves of wheat roll in the sun.
Where the big and burly bison run
under a sky in constant change.
Let's sing a song of our home on the range.

Railroads had a dramatic impact on Kansas. With its location set right in the middle of the United States, Kansas became the crossroads of America as the railroad allowed goods and people to travel west from the eastern cities. Built by Cyrus Holliday (the founder of Topeka), The Atchison, Topeka, and Santa Fe quickly became one of the great railroads in American history.

If train travel helped build old Kansas, air travel helped build modern Kansas. Perhaps it started with a simple fascination with the wide-open sky. Barnstormers used to entertain Kansans with their flying stunts high over the plains. And the aircraft industry has largely been a Kansas industry. The great aviation companies of American history (Cessna, Beech, Boeing, Lear) were founded in Kansas.

We can do a lot of traveling with our first letter A
on The Atchison, Topeka and Santa Fe.
But it's also aviation with pilots and planes galore.
Maybe the beautiful prairie sky makes Kansans want to soar.

The American Bison is better known as a buffalo. It was adopted as the Kansas State Animal in 1955.

In 1871, one single herd near Dodge City was estimated at four million buffalo. Native Americans had long relied on the buffalo for food, clothing, and shelter. But hunters and settlers wiped out the herds and threatened the very existence of one of the symbols of the Old West.

In 1891 in Springfield, Massachusetts, Dr. James Naismith nailed two peach baskets to a gymnasium wall and taught his students to toss a soccer ball into the baskets. The game of basketball was born. The game proved immediately popular and soon, Dr. Naismith came to Lawrence to become the first basketball coach at the University of Kansas. Over the years, Kansas has given the game some of its greatest coaches (Phog Allen, Adolph Rupp, and Dean Smith) and some of its greatest players (Wilt Chamberlain, Danny Manning, and Mitch Richmond).

B They once crowded the Kansas plain and stretched to the far horizon is a burly buffalo, also known as a bison.
And B is for the bushel basket nailed up on a wall,
for Kansans there's a special love for the game of basketball.

C c

From Coffeyville to Colby,
Clay Center to Chanute,
C is a colossal combine,
wheat pouring from its chute.
A C for crops, and a C for cattle.
It might not be on the label,
but think of how much Kansas
is on your dinner table!

Kansas has been called the "World's Breadbasket" due to its enormous production of wheat, wheat flour, and beef. It's estimated that one out of every five jobs in Kansas is in some way connected to agriculture.

Wheat is one of the most important grains in the world. On average, Kansas is the leading wheat producer in the United States. Every year, Kansas farmers grow enough wheat to provide every person on earth with six loaves of bread.

The Kansas beef industry traces its roots all the way back to the cowboys driving cattle to market more than a century ago. Today, Kansas is one of the leading beef producers in the United States.

Dig out your denim and a duster, too. Put on your cowboy best.
We'll find our D right here in Dodge City, center of the wild, wild West.
Here they drove cattle on the Texas trail under a frontier sun.
And good, brave men like Wyatt Earp kept outlaws on the run.

Dd

Dodge City started with a single sod house built along the Santa Fe Trail in 1871 by H.L. Sitler. The Santa Fe Railroad reached Dodge City a year later and the town quickly became a center of frontier western life. Cattle drivers brought thousands of longhorn cattle to Dodge City to load onto railcars. But cowboys weren't the only ones who came to Dodge City. The town attracted gamblers, buffalo hunters, and gunslingers.

Fortunately, lawmen like Marshall Wyatt Earp and Sheriff Bat Masterson were on hand to keep the peace. Visitors today can still find a lot of the old West on Dodge City's Front Street and in the Boot Hill Museum.

E e

Kansas has produced three NASA astronauts. After becoming the youngest Air Force officer to earn an astronaut's wings, Joe Engle of Chapman commanded the second flight of the Space Shuttle *Columbia* in 1981.

Ron Evans of St. Francis was the pilot of the Command Module on the *Apollo 17* space flight.

And Stephen Hawley of Salina is a veteran of five space flights and helped deploy the Hubble Space Telescope.

Amelia Earhart of Atchison was an aviation pioneer. Probably the most famous female aviator in history, she became the first woman to fly across the Atlantic Ocean. She was the first person to fly from Hawaii to the U.S. mainland. She was also the author of several books about her adventures. Amelia Earhart disappeared somewhere in the Pacific in 1937, trying to become the first woman to fly around the world. But her story of bravery continues to inspire today.

E is for the explorers who dared to dream of flight.
It's Joe Engle and Ron Evans, rocketing out of sight.
And it's heroic Amelia Earhart, aloft and soaring free,
becoming the first woman to fly across the sea.

As settlers started to move west on the Santa Fe Trail, forts were built across Kansas to protect them. Two of the forts remain active today. Fort Leavenworth is the oldest continuously operating U.S. Army fort west of the Mississippi River. And Fort Riley has a rich history that reaches back to its days as headquarters of the United States Cavalry.

Kansas was profoundly shaped by the debate over slavery. In the mid 1800s, many lives were lost in fighting between *abolitionists* who wanted Kansas to be a free state and those who wanted Kansas to be a state where landowners could keep slaves. The term "Bleeding Kansas" refers to the fierce and bloody battles over the issue. Kansas finally entered the Union on January 29, 1861 as a free state, and nearly two-thirds of the state's men fought for the Union in the Civil War. Those who supported the Union were known as jayhawkers, a nickname that remains with the state today.

Ff

F is for the forts that guard the Kansas plains,
        built to protect the pioneers in westward wagon trains.
    And F is also freedom. Let it live in lasting glory
        that the fight to keep all people free is the heart of the Kansas story.

Wild Bill Hickok was one of the most famous characters of the Old West. He was a scout for the Union Army in the Civil War. He then became a lawman in Kansas and helped bring law and order to frontier towns like Hays City, Fort Riley, and Abilene. In 1876, he was killed while playing cards. The hand that he was holding of black aces and eights has been known ever since as a "dead man's hand."

Buffalo Bill Cody started down the road to western fame as a rider for the Pony Express. Like Wild Bill, he was a scout for the Union Army. After the war, he began hunting buffalo to feed the workers on the mighty Kansas Pacific Railroad. He was an expert shot which earned him the nickname "Buffalo Bill." He created "Buffalo Bill's Wild West," a traveling show which brought him worldwide fame. For a while, the show included his friend Wild Bill Hickok.

Gg

A **G** for giddy-up and a gallop through the past
for the giant Kansas legends on horses trim and fast.
Men like Wild Bill Hickok, charging up a hill,
and William Frederick Cody, better known as Buffalo Bill.

H h

A great big **H** for Hutchinson, home of the Kansas State Fair.
H is also for Harvey House, for you may not be aware
that Fred Harvey thought most restaurants served their food too slow.
Think of that the next time you're asked, "Would you like your order to go?"

The Kansas State Fair traces its roots back to a two-day fair in a small Hutchinson stable in 1873. Today, people come from all over the state every September to enjoy the rides and entertainers and celebrate the state's agricultural heritage.

In many ways, Fred Harvey invented "fast food." In the late 1800s, train travelers didn't have many choices for meals. But Fred Harvey caused a sensation when he opened his first Harvey House restaurant in the Topeka depot. When trains approached, a huge gong was rung and the cooks and waitresses would swing into action, trying to prepare meals that could be eaten during the quick station stop. The speedy service and hot, tasty food created an entirely new approach to the restaurant business. And the waitresses, known as "Harvey Girls," were a nationally known symbol of hospitality.

The railroads gave birth to many hotels and restaurants including the Brookville Hotel, still serving chicken dinners today in Abilene.

Dwight D. Eisenhower was born in Texas in 1890, but his family soon moved to Abilene where Dwight spent his childhood. A terrific young athlete, Dwight chose the life of a soldier and accepted an appointment to West Point. During World War II, he was the supreme commander of one of the largest armies ever assembled.

After the war, he was immensely popular. And his nickname had the entire nation saying, "I like Ike." That campaign slogan led to the White House in 1953. His two terms are remembered as a period of calm and peace for the United States.

I is also for interstate. As President, Dwight Eisenhower created the Interstate Highway System.

I i

A little boy from Abilene, do you think that anyone knew
that he'd grow up to lead the way to winning World War II?
I is for Ike, that Kansas boy who grew to hold such power,
the 34th President of the United States, Dwight D. Eisenhower.

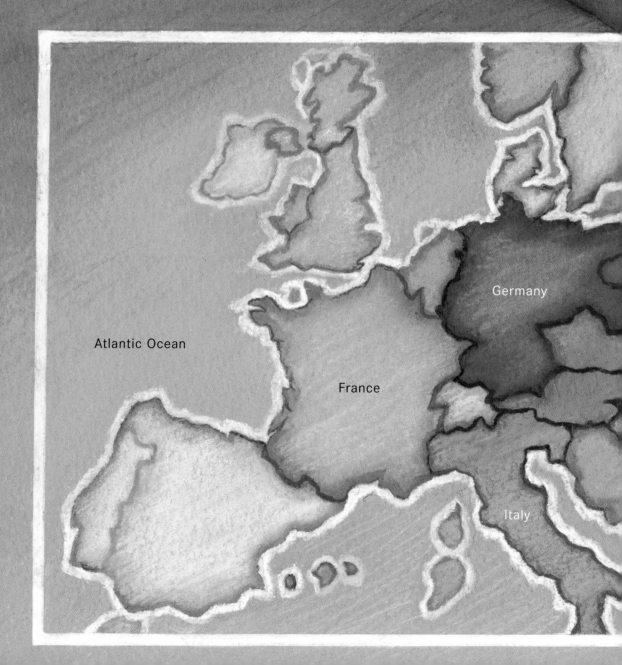

Russia

I LIKE IKE

Feel that beat, that American tune with style and such pizzazz.
J The most American sound of all is the swinging sound of jazz.
So a jiving **J** for the Kansas legends playing a jazzy ditty,
like Coleman Hawkins and Charlie Parker, jamming in Kansas City.

J j

Kansas City is one of several American cities that were key hubs in the development of jazz music.

Before a young Kansan named Coleman Hawkins came along, jazz bands had little use for the saxophone. But Hawkins almost single-handedly changed that, becoming the first great jazz sax soloist.

About the time Hawkins was playing in the Topeka High School band, Charlie Parker was born in Kansas City, Kansas in 1920. As a boy, he was disappointed when a teacher assigned him to play tuba. He taught himself the saxophone instead and millions of jazz fans are glad he did. In creating a new kind of jazz called "be-bop," Charlie (known to many as "Bird") was one of the most influential American artists of all time.

Count Basie was another great Kansas City jazzman. He was a traveling musician who ran out of money in Kansas City. Unable to return home, he stayed put and helped create the Kansas City sound.

K k

Kansas City, Kansas and Kansas City, Missouri are divided by the Missouri River. When people speak of Kansas City, they can mean either one or both!

From its start as a small trading post on the river, Kansas City has grown into a cosmopolitan metropolis. The railroads helped build Kansas City into a capital of the cattle industry. In 1870, the Kansas City Stockyards opened, cementing Kansas City as one of the world's leading cattle centers. To many visitors a trip to Kansas City wouldn't be complete without a meal of Kansas City steak at one of the city's legendary steakhouses.

But Kansas City is also famous for barbecue and you can start quite an argument by asking a group of people, "Which Kansas City restaurant serves the best barbecue in town?"

And Kansas City gives us K, though one city's really two.
With one in Kansas and one in Missouri, there's twice as much to do.
Whether it's beef or barbecue, the food is worth the trip.
So settle in with a knife and fork and a Kansas City strip.

Laura Ingalls Wilder had no idea she was writing a classic when she wrote *Little House on the Prairie*. She simply wanted to tell people about the life of the pioneers, the same life she had lived as a little girl growing up in Kansas, Wisconsin, Minnesota, and South Dakota. Her books about prairie living have been translated into 40 languages and a very popular TV series. South of the town of Independence, you can visit a reconstructed log cabin built on the site where Laura lived as a child.

Langston Hughes was born in 1902 and grew up in Lawrence and Topeka. He was an important part of an African-American artistic movement that celebrated black life and culture. In poems, novels, essays and even children's books, he spoke out powerfully against racism and intolerance.

A pioneer family, in a home on the plains can sound rather ordinary.
L   But not in Laura Ingalls Wilder's *Little House on the Prairie*.
And an L for Langston, as in Langston Hughes, truly one of a kind.
Helping the world understand the African-American mind.

M
m

In 1925, Kansans voted on an official state bird. The meadowlark, the bobwhite quail, the cardinal, and the prairie chicken were nominated. The meadowlark won, but it wasn't officially adopted until 1937 (along with the cottonwood tree as the state's official tree). The meadowlark is known for its beautiful, melodic song.

Milford Lake is located in Geary County near Junction City. Built by the Army Corps of Engineers in the 1960s, it's popular with fisherman, boaters, and campers.

Raised on a Kansas farm near Sharon in Barber County, Martina McBride took her powerful voice to Nashville and sang her way to stardom in country music.

We're off to Kansas' largest lake. Lake Milford gives us M.
Another M for the meadowlark, singing his morning hymn.
Our state bird's song is sweet and pure, the sign of a Kansas spring.
Maybe hearing the meadowlark made Martina McBride want to sing.

N is for Native Americans, of today and long ago.
To them the land was paradise with its sea of buffalo.
"The People of the South Wind," were here when settlers came.
So salute the Kansa Indians who gave the state its name.

The Kansa Indians took their name from a Sioux word meaning "People of the South Wind." With its huge herds of buffalo and vast grazing lands, Kansas was a perfect home for tribes like the Pawnee, the Wichita, the Osage, and the Comanche.

When the first Europeans arrived there were already several groups of Plains Indians living here. When explorer Francisco de Coronado came through the southwest, he was told that he would find a city of gold called "Quivera" in Kansas. It may have been that the Native Americans were simply sending Coronado on a fruitless scavenger hunt for riches, but all he found were the Quivera Indians who lived in grass lodges made from tall prairie grasses.

Haskell Indian Nations University, designed especially for Native American students, is in Lawrence.

Charles Curtis of Topeka was the Vice President under Herbert Hoover, the first and only Native American to hold such office.

n
N

Kansas has produced many great athletes over the years, many of them in track and field. Al Oerter won the gold medal in the discus in four straight Olympic Games. Maurice Green raced to gold in the 100 meters in Sydney in 2000. Other track greats include runner Glenn Cunningham, shot putters John Kuck and Bill Neider, and Jim Ryun who set a world record in the mile run and later became a U.S. Congressman.

Many Kansas basketball players have played in the Olympics, including Lynette Woodard of Wichita, who was also the first woman to play for the Harlem Globetrotters.

Native American Billy Mills came out of Haskell Institute in 1964 to shock the world in becoming the first American ever to win gold in the 10,000 meter run. His win was such a surprise that a reporter ran up to him after the race and asked, "Who are you?" His marvelous story became a movie called "Running Brave."

Look at the O's in the Olympic rings. O is for olympiad.
Kansans have been among the greatest the games have ever had.
The strength of Al Oerter, Lynette Woodard's grace, the way that Billy Mills ran
And drape a gold medal on Maurice Green, the world's fastest man.

P p

In 1958, pizza was becoming a popular food in the United States. Two brothers at Wichita State University thought the craze might last. Frank and Dan Carney opened their restaurant in a small building in Wichita. Since only nine letters would fit on the sign out front, the Carneys decided to call their restaurant Pizza Hut.

The popular pie led to another Pizza Hut in Topeka and soon, the red roofs of Pizza Hut restaurants were found all over the country. Today, travelers around the world can find a taste of home in Pizza Huts from Australia to China to Great Britain. In fact, the Pizza Hut restaurant that sells the most pizza isn't in the United States; it's the Pizza Hut in Paris.

Gordon Parks of Fort Scott overcame poverty and prejudice to become a world-renowned photographer, writer, and filmmaker.

A **P** for all the Pizza Huts. They're such a common sight.
And there's a little bit of Kansas in each and every bite.
And a great big P for Gordon Parks. His camera and his pen
showed the world a man is more than the color of his skin.

The bobwhite quail is easily recognized by his signature call of "*bob-bob-white!*" Quail are very social birds traveling in groups known as bevies. When roosting at night, they gather in a circle facing outward with their tail-feathers together to stay warm. A sudden noise or disturbance will send the bevy scattering in all directions.

One million years ago, the plains of Kansas were covered by an enormous inland sea. Prehistoric life flourished and left its imprint in fossils that can be found in Kansas limestone. One of the most noted landmarks left behind is Castle Rock, a tall tower of limestone standing over the prairie of Gove County near Quinter that can be seen for miles. Erosion and gravity continue to reshape Castle Rock some 80 million years in the making.

Q q

You'll find our Q in Kansas fields, with its brown, speckled tail.
Rustle the brush and straight for the sky flies a bevy of bobwhite quail.
And head to Quinter for a tower of stone, quite a sight you'll agree.
The Castle Rock is standing guard, left over from an ancient sea.

Rr

A flag of blue and crimson; a banner of purple satin.
   One proudly waves in Lawrence, the other in Manhattan.
R is a raucous rivalry. What kind of fan are you?
   Do you cheer for the Cats of Kansas State or the Hawks of old K.U.?

Founded in 1863, Kansas State University is located in Manhattan. Its teams are nicknamed the "Wildcats." The team colors are purple and white. It's also known as K-State or K.S.U.

Founded one year later, the University of Kansas is located in Lawrence. Its teams are nicknamed the "Jayhawks." The team colors are crimson and blue. It's also known as K.U.

There are several other proud schools in Kansas, including Wichita State, Emporia State, Ft. Hays State, Pittsburg State, and Washburn University, located in Topeka.

An **S** for a stand of sunflowers, swaying in the sun.
Take a look at the Kansas flag and you'll find another one.
Lovely and bright, but rugged and tough. Sound like someone you know?
The yellow sunflower is very much like the people who live in its glow.

The state flower of Kansas wasn't always appreciated. In the late 1800s, the sunflower was declared a troublesome weed and there was an attempt to clear it from the Kansas soil. But the flower proved too tough and many began to appreciate both its sunny beauty and its resilience. In 1903 it became the official state flower of Kansas.

The sunflower isn't just a pretty face; it's also sought for its oil and, of course, for sunflower seeds!

AD ASTRA PER ASPERA

Topeka became the capital of Kansas when Kansas became a state. In its territorial days, Ft. Leavenworth, Shawnee Mission, Pawnee, Lecompton, Minneola, Leavenworth and Lawrence all served as capitals.

The capitol building in Topeka is enormous, standing a few feet taller than the United States Capitol in Washington, DC. In the Kansas capitol building, you'll find the flags of several nations. England, France, Mexico, Spain, and the Republic of Texas all claimed parts of Kansas at one time or another. But the United States flag added its 34th star when Kansas became a state in 1861.

The winds in a tornado can reach 250 miles per hour. Kansas sits in the middle of so-called "Tornado Alley." Thunderstorms can spawn huge towers of violent, swirling winds that can cause severe damage to homes, people, and crops. Because tornado watches and warnings are so frequent, Kansas children learn tornado safety at a very young age.

Tt

A capital T for a capital town. The governor calls it home. A capital T for Topeka and its towering copper dome.
And T is for tornado. Every Kansas school child knows where to go and what to do when the tornado siren blows.

U is for the umber color the prairie grass turns in fall
under a sky of ultramarine in summer's curtain call.
   It's the understated beauty of the Flint Hills at dawn,
the golden plains where earth and sky go on and on and on…

A Kansas field can be a cornucopia of grasses and wildflowers. At one time, 400,000 square miles of tallgrass prairie covered North America in perfect grazing lands. Today, about one percent of it is left and most of it is in the Flint Hills of Kansas. There are only four such prairies left in the world.

In 1996, the Tallgrass Prairie National Preserve was created. How important are prairies grasses to Kansas? Keep in mind that wheat is just one of the many varieties of grass.

U u

V

v

Immigrants came to Kansas to try and build new lives on the rich Kansas soil. Many came from Germany and created all-German towns like Ellinwood.

Many Swedish immigrants came to Kansas and landed in Lindsborg, a city that still celebrates its Swedish heritage today.

The Volga Germans actually came to Kansas from Russia and brought with them Turkey Red Wheat. Turkey Red was perfectly suited for the Kansas climate and soil and helped Kansas become the wheat state it is now.

Kansas towns love to celebrate their immigrant heritage. In many festivals and fairs, you can sample immigrant Kansan food like Russian beirocks (meat and cabbage stuffed into dough), Swedish meatballs, and German sausages.

V is for the visitors who came and decided to stay.
They came from all over Europe and changed the Kansas way.
They brought us brand new customs and brand new foods to eat,
just like the Volga Germans, who brought a brand new wheat.

Wichita is the largest city in Kansas. A center of the aviation industry, it's nick-named "The Air Capital of the World." It's home to the Kansas Aviation Museum which chronicles the rich history of Kansans who pioneered flight.

When Susan Madora Salter was elected mayor of Argonia in 1887, she became the first woman mayor in the United States. In 1926, Mabel Chase became the first woman in the United States to be elected sheriff.

With her performance in "Gone With the Wind," Hattie McDaniel of Wichita became the first African-American woman to win an Academy Award.

When President Harry Truman appointed her in 1949, Georgia Neese Clark Gray of Richland became the first woman named United States Treasurer.

When Nancy Landon Kassebaum became a U.S. Senator in 1978, she was the only woman in the Senate.

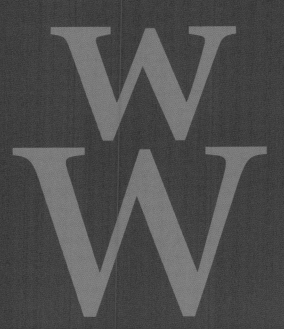

Think of the city of Wichita next time you're in the air.
The city's airplane makers might have put you there.
And W stands for women, so many pioneers,
the wonderful Kansas women who forged new frontiers.

X x

Draw an **X** on the U.S.A., on the lower 48.
You'll find the lines will meet right here in our very central state.
It's near the town of Lebanon that X will come to rest,
the exact geographic center of the continental U.S.

About four miles west of Lebanon, you'll find the monument marking the spot. Stand there and you're standing on the exact center of the United States, not including Alaska and Hawaii. (In case you're interested, if you include the two, the exact center of the country moves to a remote spot in South Dakota).

Anytime you see someone using surveying equipment, they're taking measurements that are based on a Kansas location. The Geodetic Center was placed in 1891 just southeast of Osborne, Kansas. It's the initial point upon which all North American surveys and maps are based.

Frank Baum's *The Wizard of Oz* appeared in 1900 and immediately, Americans were swept away by the adventures of Dorothy, her dog Toto, the Scarecrow, the Tin Man, and the Cowardly Lion. The 1939 film is one of the most beloved and popular movies in American history.

After the first book sold a million copies in just one year, Baum wrote several more *Oz* books. He tried to end the series after the sixth book, but heartbroken readers convinced him to continue the stories, which he did with 15 *Oz* books in all. After his death in 1919, Ruth Plumly Thompson wrote another 18 books of *Oz* adventures, followed by several other authors bringing the total to 40.

For people in other parts of the country, the state of Kansas and *The Wizard of Oz* go together like, well... like Dorothy and Toto.

Yy

A Kansas girl in ruby slippers.
A witch as green as a toad.
Y We're off to see *The Wizard of Oz*.
is for yellow brick road.
Oz was lovely, but Dorothy found no matter where she'd roam,
she'd much prefer her Kansas farm,
for "There's no place like home!"

A zephyr is a wind that comes out of the west. Kansas is one of the windiest states in the country. Chicago, Illinois is nicknamed "The Windy City," but Dodge City, Kansas is actually the windiest city in the nation. Every day the wind blows at an average of 14 miles per hour.

Wind can be turned into electricity, which makes Kansas a kind of natural power plant. In western Kansas, wind is plentiful enough to be farmed. Huge windmills, or turbines, are built on vast open fields known as "wind farms." The wind turns the giant turbines, which then turn the energy of the wind into electrical power. Wind is a great energy source since it doesn't spread any pollutants into the air or ground.

Zz

On a classic Kansas day, you'll fly your kite with ease,
zipping through the blue on the zesty Kansas breeze.
Z is for zephyr, a Kansas zephyr, making the windmills go,
for seldom comes a Kansas day when the wind doesn't blow.

A Breadbasket Full of Kansas Facts

1. What is the state animal of Kansas?

2. This Kansas native was the first woman to fly across the Atlantic Ocean. What is her name?

3. Dwight D. Eisenhower spent his childhood in Abilene. He later went on to hold an important position for our country. Who was he?

4. These two cities share the same name but are in different states. Name them.

5. Our state bird is known for its beautiful, melodic song. What is our state bird?

6. This tall tower of limestone standing near Quinter can be seen for miles and is a landmark of prehistoric life in Kansas. What is the name of this landmark?

7. Why wasn't our state flower always appreciated?

8. Name the capital city of Kansas.

9. Wichita is not only the largest city in Kansas; it is also a leader of industry. What is its nickname?

10. About four miles west of Lebanon there is a monument marking a particular spot. What is this spot?

11. Founded in the late 1800s, this Kansas town quickly became a center for Wild West life. It's also the windiest city in the nation. Name this city.

12. Kansas City music legend Charlie Parker is famous for creating a new kind of jazz music. What is it called?

13. This beloved children's story featured a young Kansas girl and her little dog and their adventures in a strange land. What is the name of the story and who wrote it?

14. After he invented this popular sport by tossing a soccer ball through peach baskets nailed to a gym wall, Dr. James Naismith moved to Kansas to become a coach at the University of Kansas. What sport did he invent?

15. Why is Kansas called the "World's Breadbasket"?

Answers

1. The American Bison, better known as a buffalo, is the state animal of Kansas.

2. Amelia Earhart of Atchison was the first woman to fly across the Atlantic Ocean.

3. Dwight D. Eisenhower became the 34th president of the United States.

4. The cities are Kansas City, Kansas and Kansas City, Missouri, and they are divided by the Missouri River.

5. The meadowlark

6. Castle Rock

7. In the late 1800s, the sunflower was considered to be a troublesome weed and there was an attempt to clear it from the Kansas soil.

8. Topeka

9. A center of the aviation industry, it's nick-named "The Air Capital of the World."

10. The exact geographic center of the continental U.S.

11. Dodge City

12. Be-bop

13. The *Wizard of Oz* was written by Frank Baum.

14. He invented the sport of basketball.

15. Kansas has earned this nickname due to its enormous production of wheat, wheat flour, and beef. Kansas is the leading wheat producer in the United States.

Devin & Corey Scillian

Born and raised in Junction City, Corey Scillian received her master's degree in education at the University of Kansas and has gone on to pursue her interest in pottery. Born at Ft. Riley, Devin is also a graduate of K.U. and anchors the news for the NBC affiliate in Detroit. His other books include the national bestseller *A is for America*. The Scillians live in Michigan with their four children, Griffin, Quinn, Christian, and Madison.

Doug Bowles

Doug Bowles is a graduate of the Columbus College of Art & Design in Columbus, Ohio and has been a freelance illustrator for 20 years. He enjoys working with a wide range of clients in advertising, corporate, editorial communities, and in the children's book market. His work has been selected many times in the Society of Illustrators West competition, and he has had several gallery showings. Doug lives in Leawood, Kansas with his wife and two children.